Gila Monsters

DISCOVER

Thanks for checking out the DISCOVER Books Series. Please note: All Rights Reserved. No part of this publication may be reproduced in any form or by any means, including scanning, photocopying, or otherwise without prior written permission of the copyright holder. Copyright © 2014

Gila Monsters

The Gila Monster (pronounced HEE-la) is one of the most feared reptiles in the world. There are many myths that swirl around this creature (which we will explore later). The Gila Monster is a very interesting creature. In fact, in this book we are going to discover all sorts of cool facts about Gila Monster. We will explore things like where it can be found, its extraordinary abilities and much more. Read on to be totally amazed with this strange creature.

Where in the World?

Did you know the Gila monster is found in the Southwestern United States and Mexico? Its range also includes Sonora, Arizona, parts of California, Nevada, Utah, and New Mexico. People in these regions have no need to fear the Gila monster. Read on to discover more...

Myths of the Gila Monster

Did you know this lizard is very misunderstood? The Gila is often feared because of the many myths attached to it. Folklore has told people that this lizard can spit its venom and leap several feet in the air to attack. It is also said this lizard can sting with its tongue and kill people with gusts of its poisonous breath.

Habitat of the Gila Monster

Did you know this lizard likes to inhabit scrubland? It can also be found in the succulent desert and oak woodland. It looks for shelter in burrows, thickets and under rocks. These areas usually are close to places with moisture. In fact, Gila monsters like the water, It has been seen enjoying a puddle after a big rain.

The Body of a Gila Monster

Did you know the Gila is the largest lizard in the United States? It also the only venomous one native to the US. It can measure up to 22 inches long (56 centimeters) in total length. It has distinct toes that have claws on each one. It has a thick tail that is able to store fat.

The Skin of a Gila Monster

Did you know this lizard has weird skin? The Gila monster's heavy body is covered with beadlike scales. These are called, osteoderms. It can be black and yellow or pink covering all but their belly. Some of them even have patterns and stripes on their skin.

The Bite of a Gila Monster

Did you know this lizard has enlarged, grooved teeth in its lower jaw? When it bites, its powerful jaws chew the venom into its victim. This is done through the capillaries along the grooves in its teeth. The Gila monster venom is about as toxic as that of a western diamondback rattlesnake.

What a Gila Monster Eats

Did you know the Gila monster feeds on meat? That makes it a carnivore. It preys on small birds, mammals, frogs, lizards, insects, and carrion (dead things). The Gila monster only needs to eat big meals about 5 to 10 times-a-year. This is because it has a slow metabolism. Plus, it can eat up to one-third of its body mass at one meal..

The Gila Monster's Special Ability

Did you know the Gila has a great sense of smell? This lizard has a super-sniffer. It uses this keen sense to locate prey, especially eggs; those are its favorite. It can locate and dig up eggs buried 6 inches into the ground (15 centimeters) deep. The Gila can also follow a scent-trail left behind by a rolling egg.

The Gila Monster Mom

Did you know the breeding season of the Gila is usually in early summer? The female Gila will dig a hole. She then lays a clutch (or group) of large, leathery, oval-shaped eggs in the hole. She then covers them up. Her eggs are not buried very deep, so the heat of the sun incubates them.

The Baby Gila Monster

Did you know after about four months, the baby Gila monsters break out of their eggs? Once out of the egg, they crawl to the surface. They measure about 3 inches long (7.6 centimeters). They look like mini-adult Gila monsters, except they are brightly colored. The hatchlings are on their own with no help from the parents.

Predators of the Gila Monster

Did you know this lizard is preyed upon by coyotes and raptors? The Gila prefers to be left alone. To warn off potential predators, it will open its mouth very wide and hiss. Gila monster bites are rarely fatal to humans. However, it will hurt a lot.

Life of a Gila Monster

Did you know the Gila can live to be over 20 years-old? In the wild, Gila's spend most of their lives hidden below the ground. They do this to stay safe from predators. If you want to see this lizard up close and safely, they are best to be viewed at zoos. Here they are very popular lizards.

The Banded Gila Monster

Did you know this Gila is pink, orange and red? It also has 4 or 5 black bands with spots in them running around its body. The tail is also banded. Its head is spotted with black around its eyes and mouth. The color and patterns on this Gila lets predators know it is venomous.

The Reticulate Gila Monster

Did you know this lizard is a Southern subspecies of the Gila Monster? The Reticulated Gila monster has light markings, or bands. They are broken up to form a reticulated pattern. This means it has a definite network of lines and patterns on its skin.

The Mexican Beaded

Did you know this lizard is a cousin to the Gila Monster? It is also venomous. It can be found in Mexico and Guatemala. It can grow to be between 30 to 36 inches long (76.2 to 91.4 centimeters). It can weigh from 3.5 to 6 pounds (1.5 to 2.7 kilograms). This lizard has a long life. It can live to be 30 years-old.

Quiz

Question 1: How is the Gila monster's name pronounced?

Answer 1: *Hee-La*

Question 2: Why are some people afraid of the Gila Monster?

Answer 2: Because of all the myths around it and because it is venomous

Question 3: How big can the Gila grow?

Answer 3: 22 inches or 56 centimeters long22 inches or 56 centimeters long

Question 4: What is the Gila Monster's special ability?

Answer 4: It has a keen sense of smell

Question 5: Do the parent Gila Monster's help raise the young?

Answer 5: No. They are left on their own to survive

Thank you for checking out another title from DISCOVER Books! Make sure to check out Amazon.com for many other great books.

Made in United States
Troutdale, OR
06/24/2025

32349477R00019